MAY   2018

Earth's Environment in Danger

Oil Drilling and Fracking

Kenneth Adams

PowerKiDS press

New York

Published in 2018 by The Rosen Publishing Group, Inc.
29 East 21st Street, New York, NY 10010

First Edition

Editor: Elizabeth Krajnik
Book Design: Rachel Rising

Photo Credits: Cover, p. 5 Calin Tatu/Shutterstock.com; cover, pp. 1, 3, 4, 6, 8, 10, 12, 14, 16, 18, 20, 22, 23, 24 (background) ALKRO/Shutterstock.com; p. 6 Hulton Archive/Getty Images; p. 7 hiroshi teshigawara/Shutterstock.com; p. 8 nata-lunata/Shutterstock.com; p. 9 panco971/Shutterstock.com; p. 11 Lukasz Z/Shutterstock.com; p. 13 Lonny Garris/Shutterstock.com; p. 14 SAPhotog/Shutterstock.com; p. 15 John Gomez/Shutterstock.com; p. 16 https://commons.wikimedia.org/wiki/File:Lake_Side_Power_Plant.jpg; pp. 17, 19 Bloomberg/Getty Images; p. 18 Photo Image/Shutterstock.com; p. 20 Tom Williams/CQ-Roll Call Group/Getty Images; p. 21 Matthew D White/ Photolibrary/Getty Images; p. 22 Sira Anamwong/Shutterstock.com.

Cataloging-in-Publication Data

Names: Adams, Kenneth.
Title: Oil drilling and fracking / Kenneth Adams.
Description: New York : PowerKids Press, 2018. | Series: Earth's environment in danger | Includes index.
Identifiers: LCCN ISBN 9781538326138 (pbk.) | ISBN 9781538325438 (library bound) | ISBN 9781538326145 (6 pack)
Subjects: LCSH: Petroleum industry–Environmental aspects. | Fossil fuels–Environmental aspects–Juvenile literature. | Petroleum engineering–Juvenile literature. | Hydraulic fracturing–Juvenile literature.
Classification: LCC TD195.P4 A33 2018 | DDC 333.8'230973–dc23

Manufactured in the United States of America

CPSIA Compliance Information: Batch #BW18PK: For Further Information contact Rosen Publishing, New York, New York at 1-800-237-9932

Contents

We Need Energy

We need energy to light and heat our homes and businesses and to make our cars and planes go. Energy is found in all **organic** matter—including trees, animals, and humans. However, not all energy is created equally. Over time, oil and natural gas, which are types of fuel, formed inside the earth.

Humans have been taking these fuels from the earth, burning them, and making use of the energy they give off for thousands of years. Today, humans drill for oil and search to find natural gas. However, these practices often harm the **environment**.

[Danger Alert!]

Around 500 BC, the Chinese took gas that leaked out of the earth and used it to boil seawater to make drinking water.

Oil and natural gas come from deep inside the earth. In order to get them out, people must use large machines.

Black Gold

Crude oil is a **fossil fuel** formed from dead plants and animals that once lived in the shallow seas that covered the earth millions of years ago. Over time, the organic matter sunk to the seafloor, mixed with sand and dirt, and was buried. Millions of years of pressure from sand, dirt, and rock above it and high temperatures turned the matter into crude oil.

Petroleum, which is another name for crude oil, is found in **reservoirs** where these ancient seas used to be. There are reservoirs under the earth's surface and beneath the seafloor.

John D. Rockefeller

[Danger Alert!]

Crude oil is called black gold because it's very valuable. Selling oil is what made John D. Rockefeller one of the richest people of all time.

Crude oil is usually black or dark brown. However, some crude oil can be yellow, red, tan, or green.

Using Crude Oil

People have been using crude oil since ancient times. Some early groups of people used crude oil to waterproof their boats. However, people have only used oil in the same way we use it today for less than 200 years. In 1859, Edwin Drake drilled nearly 70 feet into the earth and struck oil in Titusville, Pennsylvania.

Since Drake's discovery, people have used crude oil for many purposes. Crude oil can be **refined** to make gasoline, jet and diesel fuel, and kerosene, a type of fuel. It may also be part of medicines, makeup, paint, pens, and plastic bottles.

gasoline

Plastic bottles often end up in Earth's rivers, lakes, and oceans. The Great Pacific Garbage Patch is mostly made up of plastics.

Oil and Water

In 1983, President Ronald Reagan claimed the 200 miles off the shores of the United States as part of the exclusive economic zone, or EEZ. Today, all countries that border the sea have an EEZ of 200 miles from their coastlines.

If oil reservoirs are discovered within a country's EEZ, the country may choose to drill wells in the ocean floor to let the oil flow out. Large rigs sit at the surface of the water and are connected to a drill that digs into the ocean floor. Some of these oil rigs are so big that hundreds of people can live and work on them.

[Danger Alert!]

One of the issues linked to offshore oil drilling is keeping the oil inside the pipes that carry it from the ocean floor to the surface. If these pipes break, ocean waters can become polluted.

Oil rigs can be some of the biggest offshore **structures** on Earth.

Hydraulic Fracturing

Fracking refers to **hydraulic** fracturing. This is the process of drilling into the earth to extract, or draw out, petroleum or natural gas. In fracking, water, chemicals, and sand are forced into cracks in **shale** rock formations.

Fracking **fluid** is pushed into the ground at such a high pressure that it causes the shale rock formations to fracture, or break. When the shale fractures, the natural gas or oil is released. It's pumped back up to Earth's surface through a well. Natural gas or oil is then separated from the fracking fluid that comes back to the surface.

[Danger Alert!]

The Bakken shale formation is one of the most active sites of fracking for oil. This shale formation stretches from western North Dakota and Montana to the southern part of the Canadian **province** of Saskatchewan.

Fracking sites can be close to where people live and work or farther away from populated areas, such as this site in Colorado.

Fracking Fluid

Fracking fluid is what makes it possible for people to extract natural gas from shale rock formations. It increases the amount of natural gas or petroleum that can be taken from a well. It also helps keep the well in good working condition. Fracking fluid prevents bacteria from growing, prevents the well from clogging, and allows the drill to move back and forth easily.

The U.S. government doesn't require companies to list the chemicals in fracking fluid. The chemicals change from one well to the next. However, many of these chemicals are very harmful to humans and animals.

shale rock formations

Many people protest fracking in their area because they now understand just how dangerous it can be. Fracking fluid can pollute local drinking water and put people and animals in harm's way. Some countries have banned fracking.

Using Natural Gas

Natural gas can be found in many places. Because it's easy to find, natural gas is one of the cheapest fossil fuels we use today. In the United States, people use natural gas to heat their homes, power their stoves and ovens, dry their clothing, and create electricity.

Many people think that burning natural gas is better for the environment because it burns cleaner than other fossil fuels. However, like all fossil fuels, burning natural gas harms the environment. Just like oil, natural gas releases harmful carbon dioxide into the **atmosphere** when burned.

Lake Side Power Plant, natural gas power station, Vineyard, Utah

16

In recent years, many states have entered the fracking market. This has created many jobs.

Case Study: DAPL

The Dakota Access Pipeline, or DAPL, has been the source of large-scale disagreements in the recent past. The $3.7 billion pipeline project spans close to 1,200 miles (1,931 km) across four states and can carry about 470,000 barrels of crude oil each day. The DAPL makes it cheaper to **transport** crude oil.

People joined together in Washington, D.C., on March 10, 2017, to protest the DAPL. The protesters hoped to protect Native American **sovereignty**, keep fossil fuels in the ground, and stop the construction of the DAPL.

Oceti Sakowin camp near
Standing Rock Sioux reservation

However, one part of the DAPL comes dangerously close to the Standing Rock Sioux reservation. Tribe members claimed that the DAPL would pollute their drinking water and damage sites important to their tribe. The Sioux and their supporters protested the DAPL in Washington, D.C., and around the United States.

Keeping Watch

In the United States, the Environmental Protection Agency (EPA) exists to keep watch over natural gas extraction and oil drilling and make sure that these practices don't harm the environment. The EPA also does studies on fracking and how it affects drinking water. EPA employees read published articles, look over information, and create models.

The EPA also reported on the 2010 Deepwater Horizon oil spill. This oil spill, which happened when the oil rig called Deepwater Horizon exploded and sank, is one of the largest offshore oil spills in history. From April 20, 2010, to July 15, 2010, about 4 million barrels of oil spilled from the well.

Cleanup from the Deepwater Horizon spill continued for more than eight months after the spill. The U.S. government fined the oil company BP, which owned the rig, for damages caused by the spill. Many animals were affected by the spill and needed to be cleaned off before they could be released into the wild.

What Can You Do?

One of the best ways you can fight the use of crude oil and natural gas is to educate yourself on different energy sources you can use instead of fossil fuels. Ask your parents if your home uses solar panels. Is there a wind farm near you? These could be the source of your electricity.

Another way you can get involved is to join protests against oil drilling and fracking. By showing that you don't support these practices, you can band together with other people who feel the same way. Soon, more laws against oil drilling and fracking may be created in favor of clean energy sources like wind power and solar power.

PROTEST!

Glossary

atmosphere: The whole mass of air that surrounds Earth.

environment: The conditions that surround a living thing and affect the way it lives.

fluid: A substance that flows freely like water.

fossil fuel: A fuel—such as coal, oil, or natural gas—that is formed in the earth from dead plants or animals.

hydraulic: Having to do with using water under pressure to do work.

organic: Relating to or taken from living things.

province: Any one of the large parts some countries, such as Canada, are divided into.

refine: To remove the unwanted substances in something.

reservoir: A place where a liquid is stored.

shale: A soft kind of rock that splits easily into flat pieces.

sovereignty: Independence.

structure: A building or other object that is constructed.

transport: To carry from one place to another.

Index

Websites

Due to the changing nature of Internet links, PowerKids Press has
developed an online list of websites related to the subject of this book.
This site is updated regularly. Please use this link to
access the list: www.powerkidslinks.com/eeid/fracking